Spring Training

SPORTS DEVOTIONAL

Elliot Johnson

SPRING TRAINING

ELLIOT JOHNSON

ISBN: 1-929478-44-5

CROSS TRAINING PUBLISHING
317 WEST SECOND STREET
GRAND ISLAND, NE 68801
(308) 384-5762

THIS BOOK IS MANUFACTURED IN THE UNITED STATES OF
AMERICA.

PUBLISHED BY CROSS TRAINING PUBLISHING,
317 WEST SECOND STREET
GRAND ISLAND, NE 68801

CONTENTS

Introduction • 5

An Overview of Romans • 7

Chapter One • 9
  Setting the Tempo
Chapter Two • 11
  Attitude of a Champion
Chapter Three • 13
  "Sinnerama"
Chapter Four • 15
  Educated and Moral — But Lost
Chapter Five • 17
  Religious, But Lost
Chapter Six • 19
  The Indictment
Chapter Seven • 21
  The Test
Chapter Eight • 23
  Stop Trying So Hard!
Chapter Nine • 25
  Salvation: Reward or Gift?
Chapter Ten • 27
  The Results of Being Justified
Chapter Eleven • 29
  A Line Drive
Chapter Twelve • 31
  Reconciliation
Chapter Thirteen • 33
  Adam's Fumble and Christ's Recovery
Chapter Fourteen • 35
  Dead Men Walking
Chapter Fifteen • 37
  Two Leaders

Chapter Sixteen • 39
    Marriage and Professional Players
Chapter Seventeen • 41
    "Sic 'em, Spirit"
Chapter Eighteen • 44
    Eager Expectation
Chapter Nineteen • 46
    His Followers Can't Lose!
Chapter Twenty • 48
    Super Winners
Chapter Twenty-One • 50
    God's Sovereign Choice
Chapter Twenty-Two • 52
    Enthusiastically Wrong
Chapter Twenty-Three • 54
    The Plan
Chapter Twenty-Four • 56
    Transformation
Chapter Twenty-Five • 58
    Body Parts
Chapter Twenty-Six • 60
    Character Counts
Chapter Twenty-Seven • 62
    God and Government
Chapter Twenty-Eight • 63
    Day Life or Night Life?
Chapter Twenty-Nine • 65
    Conflict Unnecessary
Chapter Thirty • 67
    Encouragement
Chapter Thirty-One • 69
    Paul's Plans
Chapter Thirty-Two • 70
    Paul — A "People Person"
Appendix I • 71
    The Winning Run
Appendix II • 75
    The Perfect Reliever

SPRING TRAINING

An Introduction to Paul's Letter to the Romans

EVERY SPRING MAJOR LEAGUE BASEBALL teams begin their season in their spring training camps in Florida and Arizona. Spring training is a time of reviewing fundamentals and players are conditioned both physically and mentally for a long season. Without the basics of spring training, a championship team is impossible.

When Paul wrote this letter to the Christians in Rome, he put every reader through "spring training" in the fundamentals of the faith. Jesus Christ had come! He had died and risen again. Multitudes had believed in Him and their lives were changed. Paul, a formerly self-righteous Pharisee (the strictest Jewish sect) was one whose life had been transformed. Even his name had been changed from Saul to Paul. A Jew among Jews, Paul was miraculously converted while on the way to Damascus to persecute Christians. Immediately, he told everyone about his conversion. This aroused much Jewish hatred of him and his story. Barely escaping with his life, Paul spent three years in the Arabian Desert south of the Dead Sea. There, God gave him direct revelation of Christian doctrine. Paul's Roman citizenship aided his travel all over the Mediterranean region, where he told whoever would listen the good news (gospel) about Jesus Christ, He was often savagely beaten by Jewish leaders who hated the message he himself had once tried to stamp out: Man could be saved from sin by doing nothing more nor less than trusting Jesus Christ to forgive them!

But now the gospel was attacked by those who twisted it as well as by those who opposed it. Some (Judaizers) said man could be kept saved only by keeping the law. Others (Antinomians) taught that a saved man could live any way he pleased. Both were in error. Around A.D. 57, Paul was in Corinth, from which he wrote to the Romans.

A Christian named Phoebe delivered it to them. Paul's purpose was to teach that the power of the gospel was sufficient to save and to keep saved all who believed in Jesus.

Rome was a great city, the single city that ruled the civilized world. Over 4.1 million people lived there. Many were slaves. Paul had never been to Rome, though he was eager to go. Beyond Rome, he desired to take the gospel to Spain (15:28). No apostle had been to Spain, either! Though Paul had never been to Rome, a sizable church had been formed by people from throughout the Roman Empire by people who had been influenced by Paul.

In Paul's letter, he defined the need of depraved man. He answers every major attitude that man can take regarding God's grace and he points us all to a righteousness from God as the solution to our sin problem. This letter is basic "spring training" for the believer in Jesus. Augustine was converted through reading this letter. Martin Luther launched the Reformation based upon it. John Calvin called it a "passage opened" to understanding the whole Scripture. Coleridge called it the most profound writing that exists and John Bunyan's life was transformed by it. The great scientist Michael Faraday based his faith upon the truths of this letter. Let the reader be warned: Reading through the letter to the Romans has resulted repeatedly in revival of soul and spirit! You are about to begin "spring training" for another season of victory!

SPRING TRAINING
An Overview of Romans

Chapter 1
The World is in a MESS!

Chapter 2
YOU are in a mess, too!

Chapter 3
ALL are lost and NO ONE seeks God-BUT a righteousness is available!

Chapter 4
Faith has ALWAYS been credited as righteousness.

Chapter 5
You are EITHER dead in Adam OR alive in Christ!

Chapter 6
You must RECKON self to be dead. There is NO good in the OLD nature.

Chapter 7
Self is frustrating. There is NO power in the NEW nature.

Chapter 8
Power is in the SPIRIT. There is no condemnation and no separation forbelievers!

Chapters 9-11
God sovereignly CHOSE Israel, but they blew it.
He saves ANYONE who believes, yet only a remnant is saved. We don't understand truth through reason. God didn't ask our opinion when He PLANNED it all!

Chapter 12
We are LIVING Sacrifices.

Chapter 13
WAKE UP and get dressed.

Chapter 14
Conscience Matters, BUT it is unreliable.

Chapters 15-16
Go TELL everyone.

Setting the Tempo

Paul, a servant of Christ Jesus, called to be an apostle and set apart for the gospel of God.

Romans 1:1

JOE GIRARDI REJOINED the Cubs in 2000 after several years with the World Champion New York Yankees. "The attitude with the Yankees was different," he said. "When you go to spring training there, you plan to go to the World Series. The Yankees come in more prepared for spring training. They're all ready to go. There are outside distractions during the season, but there really aren't because they're all fixed on that one goal."

Just as the Yankees set the tempo for their season in spring training, Paul set the tempo for his great doctrinal letter to the Romans at the start. He began by stating who he was, for he knew himself and he knew his purpose. His Roman name, Paul, means "little." He had willingly become a slave of Jesus Christ (Jesus never forces us to serve Him) and he was therefore answerable only to Him (1 Corinthians 4:1-4). As an apostle ("one who is sent"), he had personally seen Jesus Christ. He could do miracles, even the miracle of raising the dead.

Paul's purpose was to preach the gospel ("good news") of God. The Romans used the word "gospel" in emperor worship. Town heralds began public announcements about the emperor with this word, but Paul preached the gospel of *God!* God's gospel is the good news that brings eternal salvation to all who believe it! This plan was constantly promised by Old Testament prophets from Genesis 3:15 to Malachi 4:2. Paul had received this good news by the direct revelation of God Himself! This gospel of grace ("unmerited favor") was planned and promised by the Father, accomplished by the Son on the cross, and declared by the Spirit through

Jesus' resurrection from the dead. The word declared (v. 4) means "horizoned." As the horizon sets sky apart from earth, the resurrection of Jesus clearly separates Jesus from other men, proving Him to be God's Son!

Faith in Jesus produces obedience to Him, and this letter opens and closes (16:19) with obedience. Paul says we are called to be saints. Sainthood is not conferred by a Pope or a council of men. God refers to all who believe in Jesus Christ as "saints." All God's saints habitually obey Him. We have been given grace and peace *with* God. Now, we must live by grace in the peace *of* God.

When Paul set the tempo for his letter, his desire was to keep believers in Rome from falling into heresy. Did he succeed? No! The Roman church slid the furthest from Paul's teachings! May we learn from their slide and live in grace and obedience to our risen Savior, the Lord Jesus Christ.

Attitude of a Champion

I am not ashamed of the gospel because it is the power of God for the salvation of everyone who believes: first for the Jew, then for the Gentile. For in the gospel a righteousness from God is revealed, a righteousness that is by faith from first to last, just as it is written: "The righteous will live by faith."

Romans 1:16-17

KIRK GIBSON was a champion in the 1988 World Series. His pinch-hit game-winning home run lifted the Dodgers over the A's in the Series that year. Peter Gammons wrote: "He knew what he'd done the instant the ball exploded off his bat. He raised his arm and held it aloft until he reached first base (and) then he limped around the bases as if he were straggling home from the Russian front."

The apostle Paul was a champion of faith in Jesus Christ. He had the attitude of a champion. First, he thanked God for the growing faith of believers in Rome. And he had not even been there! Their commitment was so strong that the pagan emperor Claudius expelled all Jews from Rome in a.d. 49 because of the influence of "Chrestus" (Acts 18:2)!

Second, Paul prayed for the Roman believers constantly. His prayers were not sporadic, but were specific and constant.

Third, Paul desired to encourage the Roman believers and to be encouraged by their faith. He knew they needed each other.

Fourth, Paul felt obligated to give out the gospel to those in Rome who had not heard it. He knew he owed the truth he had received to others. Rome was heir to Greek culture and learning. The Graeco-Roman world represented the civilized world. Paul was a learned man.

11

He wanted to preach Christ to the center of civilization. He also wanted to preach Christ to unlearned people (barbarians). He was undeterred by previous ridicule, criticism, or torture.

Fifth, Paul was not ashamed of the gospel. Neither ridicule, criticism, or torture could sway him. The Jews abhorred it, for it proclaimed salvation apart from the law. Educated people thought it was foolish, for it is not figured out by the intellect. The masses of pagans thought it to be intolerant, for it proclaimed that Jesus was the only way to be saved.

The gospel is the power ("dynamite") of God for salvation ("rescue" or "deliverance") from sin. It is not good advice, but good news. It compels us to face our sin, God's judgment, and our need of a Savior. It tells us not how to clean up ourselves, but what Christ has done for us. It is for everyone, yet it can be received only by faith. This faith involves our intellect (understanding), our emotions (sorrow for sin and joy over God's mercy), and our will to trust Jesus only. What good news is the gospel of God! He counts as righteous every ungodly man when we do nothing more nor less than believe Him! He seeks us and rescues us from lostness, His wrath, our ignorance, evil self-indulgence, the darkness of false religion, and from eternal torment! No wonder Paul was so excited about spreading the gospel to the world. The power of God motivated him. He had the attitude of a champion!

Read Romans 1:18-32

"Sinnerama"

The wrath of God is being revealed from heaven against all the godlessness and wickedness of men who suppress the truth by their wickedness, since what may be known about God is plain to them, because God has made it plain to them.

Romans 1:18-19

BO BELINSKY was a flamboyant playboy when he pitched for the Angels in the 1960s. He dated movie stars, stayed out all night, married and divorced, and went on alcoholic and drug binges. In 1976, he woke up under a railroad bridge with an empty bottle. But before he died on November 23,2001, Bo became a born-again Christian and joined a church in Las Vegas. "Can you imagine?" he once said. "I had to come to Las Vegas to discover Jesus Christ."

God has clearly shown Himself to the most heathen person on the face of the earth, including Bo Belinsky, you and me. Psalm 19:1 says, "The heavens declare the glory of God; the skies proclaim the work of his hands." This proclamation goes on day after day in every language! Yet, most men reject the knowledge of God and turn their backs upon the Almighty. They are without excuse. Therefore, God's wrath is revealed as He gives them over to the consequences of their sin. Occasionally, God supernaturally dispenses judgment with the flood (Genesis 7), burning sulfur raining on Sodom and Gomorrah (Genesis 19), or the earth opening up to swallow Korah's men (Numbers 16:32). But most often, He hands men over to the consequences of his sin. God never tolerates sin. He hates it!

Men have no excuse for avoiding, ignoring or denying God. No one who wanted to know God and go to His heaven will ever spend eternity in hell. The strongest,

13

most persistent urge in man is not hunger or sex. It is to know God. But when man suppresses this urge, becomes ungrateful to God and worships created things, his thinking becomes futile and he becomes a fool. This is rationalism (evolution, atheism, agnosticism) and idolatry (materialistic selfishness). Men deify reason and dethrone God. Furthermore, Paul says that to worship an idol is to actually worship a demon (1 Corinthians 10:20)!

So God lets man go his own way. What could be worse? God "hands sinful man over" (vs. 24, 26, 28) in body, soul, and spirit to his evil lifestyle "choices." Man's behavior gets progressively worse. The opposite of evolution occurs! We "devolve" into behavior lower than any animal. Animals don't kill for pleasure, but to eat. No animal has sex with those of the same sex, a crime against the natural use of the body that is the ultimate distortion of God's creative genius. It becomes impossible for such people to view anything as God intended. Their darkness is very deep and they suffer in their own bodies the "due penalty for their perversion."

Wicked men, who do not value the knowledge of God, are given over to a depraved mind full of every kind of evil. They are in slavery to their own lusts. Man then seeks poor substitutes (drug abuse, material things, prestige) to satisfy the urge for God. They become hard-hearted and past feeling (Ephesians 4:19). The theory of evolution has enormous appeal for man because he has a debased mind and he wants to explain his origin outside of God. Yet, he knows that if God created him, man is accountable to Him.

To establish an atmosphere of approval of such evil deeds is condemned by God (v. 32). So is loving sin for sin's sake. Those who do such things *know* God is displeased and *know* they deserve death, however much they seek to rationalize or legalize their evil deeds.

There is hope only in confessing and forsaking sin. Complete deliverance from homosexuality, drug use, materialism, and other evils is promised to all who believe God and obey His Word!

Educated and Moral — But Lost

. . . for at whatever point you judge the other, you are condemning yourself, because you who pass judgment do the same things.

Romans 2:1

ERIC SHAW was a physics major who was nicknamed "Professor." He won 101 games in an 11-year major league career. But he rarely seemed at peace, and he made numerous enemies. Eric got into drugs and died at the age of 37 at a drug rehabilitation center in California.

All of us have a God-given awareness of right and wrong. We may be as educated as Eric Shaw, but still be lost. We have a conscience that animals were not given. Though our standards vary, we all violate our own consciences anyway! Some say they live by the Ten Commandments, others by the Sermon on the Mount or the "Golden Rule." We are guilty by any standard we choose! We are self-condemned! We may judge others sexual sins, but lust ourselves. We judge stealing, yet covet. We condemn murder, but hate. Jesus put all these sins in the same category (Matthew 5). Though all differ in frequency and degree of sin, everyone stands guilty before a Holy God. Our ability to judge "immoral" sins in others increases our own condemnation for our "moral" sins.

It is only because of God's kind patience, designed to lead us to repentance that man is not immediately judged and sent to hell. God delays immediate destruction in spite of man's ceaseless provocation. But His wrath is being "stored up" for the Great White Throne Judgment (Revelation 20:11-15) and will be revealed against sinners for all eternity.

God's judgment is based upon truth (v. 2). Pagan philosophers, though educated, judge in a spirit of self-righteousness. But they are subjective liars. But God's judg-

15

ment is based upon complete and accurate information — not circumstantial evidence.

God judges according to man's deeds (v. 6). In other words, there are degrees of punishment in hell, just as there are degrees of rewards in heaven. All are guilty, for all have sinned (Romans 3:23). Many moral men and women ("man" is a generic term) have stubborn ("hardened" or "sclerotic") hearts which resist God's grace.

God's judgment is impartial (v. 11). All are under judgment, regardless of social position, popularity, appearance, gender, influence, wealth, or temperament. Some have His laws (Jews). They will be judged by it and found guilty. Some (non-Jews) were not given the law, but their consciences are enough to convict them. God's law is "written upon their hearts." When they repeatedly ignore the warnings of conscience, they become desensitized and the warnings stop (1 Timothy 4:2).

Jesus Christ will judge all of men's secrets (Romans 2:16; John 5:22). He knows our every idle word or thought. Only His blood can cleanse us (Hebrews 9:14). Thank God for the blood of His cross!

Religious, But Lost

You, then, who teach others, do you not teach yourself?
Romans 2:21

CHAD CURTIS was a chapel leader on some great Yankee teams. But he wanted to make sure others didn't just use God for selfish purposes. He often said, "God is not a good-luck charm. He is a life giver. Which would you rather have?" Chad made sure players understood the difference between religion and being saved!

In Chapter 1, Paul said that the unrighteous heathen are lost even though they have the light of creation. In Chapter 2, Paul said the educated, self-righteous pagan philosophers are lost even though God gave them a conscience (vs. 1-16). Now, we see that religious people (Jews) are lost even though God gave them the Law of Moses. They condemned others, but failed to "practice what they preached!"

The title "Jew" was an honorable title. Yet, some were very sinful. They hated idols, yet would sell plundered idols in business deals, just as some people today who won't drink will sell alcohol. They thought themselves superior to others, but still they failed to live up to God's standard. They relied upon a minor surgical operation (circumcision) as a symbol of separation from evil, but they had no inner reality. This made a mockery of the very idea of godliness. It resembles people today who are baptized or join a church without accepting Jesus as personal Savior! They may be religious, but they are separated from God and lost. The fact that a person is religious does not prove that he is seeking God. It proves he is running away from God and filling his emptiness with a false substitute.

What advantage was there in being Jewish? The Jews were given the Old Testament Scriptures to reveal God. The nation was in covenant agreement with God. But all that resulted was Jewish pride of ancestry, religion, and knowledge. No moral change resulted.

Man may refuse to believe the truth about God, but his unbelief doesn't change the truth (v. 4). Facts are stubborn! Rejecting them doesn't change any particle of them. The majority, even the whole world could vote against God, but God will still be true and right and every person wrong and guilty before Him! Man's sin merely confirms God's righteous truth when God proclaims him guilty. But this is certainly not to the credit of man!

Yet, God will fulfill all His promises to Israel as a nation, even though individual Jews cut themselves off from His presence by their unbelief. God has a great future for Israel. Many of His promises to the nation are unfulfilled so far. When He fulfills them, those who are religious and lost will be on the outside looking in. Only those who follow Jesus will reign with Him!

The Indictment

There is no one righteous, not even one; . . .

Romans 3:10

NORM CASH indicted himself after the fact. He had won the 1961 batting title, hitting 34 with 41 home runs and 132 RBIs. But he had used an illegal, cork-filled bat to do it. He once boasted, "I owe my success to expansion pitching, a short right-field fence, and my hollow bats."

All of us are under indictment. Paul formally indicts us with heinous crimes against a holy God. Every indictment has at least one count (specific charge). Using Old Testament references, Paul lists at least 14 counts in this short passage!

Man is in a miserable condition apart from God. All of us are sinners. God says, "Not one of us is righteous! . . . Not even one!" The curse of sin is on the entire human race. We are under sin's power and control and the resulting condemnation. No one understands God or the depth of his own sin. We are spiritually deranged and incapable of spiritual understanding (1 Corinthians 2:14). We are not well, though that is the belief of most Americans. We are not sick. We are spiritually dead! Naturally, we are as responsive to God as a corpse.

Furthermore, no one seeks God! God reaches out to man (Luke 19:10). Man is really not a "truth seeker." Jesus Christ is Truth and He is received as a free gift by God's grace. Sinners are saved by receiving Jesus Christ through believing faith, but they never search for God on their own. He *draws* men to Himself! Man is *running away* from God! We naturally seek our own interests (Philippians 2:21). Our only hope is for God to seek us (John 6:37, 44). Only when God works in our hearts does anyone seek Him (Matthew 6:33).

Verses 10-18 quote six Old Testament Scriptures describing our lost condition. Verse 12 says we have become worthless ("sour, like spoiled fruit"). We are sour and corrupted by sin. No one does anything of spiritual or eternal value on his own. We need the Great Physician, for our throats are like open graves which smell of rotting human flesh. They reveal the decay in our hearts. Our tongues carry more poison than a diamondback rattlesnake. Sugar tongued flattery and cursing of God and man is typical of sinful man. We don't have to be taught to curse or lie. Our feet swiftly carry us to evil. We leave only destruction behind us. There is no peace brought by man to this world. We have no fear (respect) of God. Man destroys everything he touches, leaving pain and suffering in his wake.

The Law of Moses (given to Israel) revealed the guilt of mankind. It can never justify man, for man cannot keep it. It simply reveals how sinful both Jews and non-Jews really are. All are under the power and penalty of sin. We are totally depraved and capable of every sin ever committed. In God's courtroom, there are no flowery speeches, muddling of issues, or discrediting of witnesses. All of us stand guilty and silent before Him. No clever lawyer, plea bargain, bribery of the judge, or passionate appeal will be successful. God's verdict is guilty." There is no law anywhere that can justify us for, like a mirror or a thermometer, the law merely points out the problem. It cannot clean us up or cure our fever. Our only hope is in the grace of God!

The Test

This righteousness from God comes through faith in Jesus Christ to all who believe.

Romans 3:22

THE GAME OF LIFE, like a semester of school, is made up of numerous tests. As a Great Teacher, God has given all of us a major exam to measure our merit on His scale of righteousness. We've all failed miserably, scoring *below* zero! Then God gave Jesus Christ, His only begotten Son, the same exam. Jesus *never* sinned, scoring 100 percent! When we believe upon the Lord Jesus Christ, God the Father does an amazing thing. He takes our test paper, erases our name, and writes the name of "Jesus" on our below zero score! Our sin was placed upon His account. Then God takes the perfectly righteous paper of Jesus and writes our name on it! His righteousness is credited to our account and He is justified in receiving us into heaven.

In every test of measuring up to God's standard of righteousness, man is an utter failure. He cannot keep God's law. He never even seeks God on his own initiative. "Sin," an archery term meaning "to miss the mark," refers to our evil nature. "Sins" refers to the wrong things we have done. What we *are* (sinners) is even worse than what we have done (sin). Any hope for salvation must come from outside ourselves!

Romans 3:21-30 reveals the source of righteousness. Jesus Christ is that Source! He is "the Lord our Righteousness" (Jeremiah 23:6). He is available totally apart from our efforts to keep the law. He didn't wait for man to seek God, for man never would seek God on his own. Man *hides* from God! He is the sacrifice of atonement (propitiation) a term Paul borrowed from pagan religious sacrifices turn away wrath of their false gods).

Righteousness from God is received by believing in

21

Jesus Christ. This offer is available to all, for all have sinned. Some are better sinners than others, but it doesn't matter. Rich or poor, black or white, industrious or lazy — all fall short. God justifies man freely ("with no prior condition") on the basis of faith. Justification is a *gift* and not a *reward*. Therefore man's boasting is eliminated. What a plan! It is God's plan and He never has had another plan! "Justified" is a legal term meaning "to be declared righteous" in God's mind. It not only means just-as-if-I'd never sinned, but also that God declares us righteous in Christ in His heavenly courtroom. We are justified freely ("without cause" on our part) in exactly the way we hated Jesus "without cause" (John 15:25). This is by God's grace. Grace means "*everything* for *nothing*" to those who don't deserve *anything!* This is through the redemption of Christ Jesus. Redemption is a business term meaning "to buy back by the payment of a price." Jesus bought us back from the slave market of sin by paying in His precious blood!

For thousands of years, it appeared that God was unjust, for He left sins unpunished. All men, including some of His choice servants (David, Moses, Solomon) sinned and no penalty was paid. Then, the cross! For the 9,000 years from Adam to Jesus, God left sins unpunished (v. 25). The Jewish sacrifices pictured the perfect sacrifice. If you want to know God, He will meet you in Jesus who satisfied both the justice and mercy of God. It was on *behalf* of all (Hebrews 2:9) but *instead* of only those who believe and receive Him (John 1:12). Do you believe and have you received Him.

The gospel is "boast-free," for we have done nothing to merit salvation. It humbles us, destroying our pride. Our only contribution to our salvation was sinning. Jesus did it all. We can take no credit for faith. We are not saved *because* of our faith but *by* faith or *through* faith. It comes from God (Exodus 2:8-9).

•

22

Stop Trying So Hard!

Do we, then, nullify the law by this faith? Not at all! Rather, we uphold the law.

Romans 3:31

ATHLETES SOMETIMES TRY too hard. This is especially detrimental when skillful actions are needed as in hitting a baseball, shooting a free throw, or hitting a golf ball. The result is forced actions that are not smooth instead of relaxed flow. The solution is relaxation and focuses upon the ball. Living by the law also results in forced, uncoordinated action in life, for we cannot keep the law!

The Law of Moses was just given orally by God at Mt. Sinai (Exodus 20), then on tablets of stone (Exodus 24), and again on a second set of stone tablets (Exodus 34). But it was given only to the Jewish nation. God's Law included moral laws, ceremonial laws, dietary laws, and ordinances. One offense meant complete guilt (James 2:10; Galatians 3:10) and ignorance was no excuse (Leviticus 5:17). Judgment was executed without mercy (Hebrews 10:28). The Law was given when Israel spurned God's grace. He delivered them from Egypt by grace and mercy, but they rebelled against Him and then said they would *do* what He commanded (Exodus 19:7-8). They sought a religion instead of a relationship. God knew His people could not keep the Law. He added it to reveal their sinfulness (Romans 3:20, 5:20) and their need of the promised Savior. Israel broke the Law before they even received a copy of it (Exodus 32:1-6)! Every sacrifice of the ceremonial law acknowledged their failure to meet God's standard and pointed to the coming of Jesus as the perfect sacrifice (Hebrews 10:1, 4). If man could keep the Law, Jesus' death would have been needless!

Law does not mix with grace any more than oil mixes with water. Man is saved by grace alone. If anyone thinks

23

he must *do* anything except believe in Jesus' death and resurrection on his behalf, he is not saved. Law puts great distance between God and man. Grace brings guilty man near to God. Law utterly condemns the best of us. Grace forgives the repentant sinner. The Law kills; Grace makes alive. Law says, "Eye for eye and tooth for tooth." Grace says, "return good for evil." Law says, "hate your enemy." Grace says, "Love your enemies." Law utterly condemns the best man; Grace justifies the worst man. Under Law the sheep dies for the shepherd; under grace the Shepherd (Jesus) died for the sheep. Law says, "the wages of sin is death; Grace says, "the gift of God is eternal life" (Romans 6:23). The Law says, "love God with all your heart, soul, mind and strength," Grace says, "We love Him because He first loved us" (1 John 4:19). 1 Corinthians 3 further contrasts law and grace. The Law was written on stone; Grace upon the heart of believing men and women. The Law is of letters; Grace of the Spirit. The Law was glorious; Grace is more glorious! Believers are not under the law, but under grace (Romans 6:14). The believer who tries to keep the law after being saved by grace has "fallen from grace" as a way of living (Galatians 5:1-6). We are to live by the grace of God, just as we were saved by the grace of God. Life under law is depending upon self to produce righteousness. Life under grace is to count self as dead and to yield to God for strength (Romans 6:11, 13). This is neither legalism nor license. It is a "law of the Spirit of life" that frees us from the "law of sin and death" (Romans 8:2). Law takes us to the grace; Grace raises us with Christ!

Paul says we "uphold the law." This means we keep it in its rightful place. It points out our sin and directs us to the Savior. That is its purpose. Then we believe upon Jesus and live by grace! As an athlete focuses upon the ball, the believer must focus upon Jesus and live gracefully. He must stop trying so hard! It's the only way to produce smooth coordinated actions in life and focus on Jesus.

Salvation: Reward or Gift?

However, to the man who does not work but trusts God who justifies the wicked, his faith is credited as righteousness.

Romans 4:5

IN 1987, THE MINNESOTA TWINS won their first American League Pennant in 22 years. Over 50,000 people crowded into the Metrodome to welcome the Twins home from their victory over Detroit which secured the flag. Banners waved and horns were blown. One reporter said to shortstop Greg Gagne, "This has got to be the greatest moment of your life." Gagne replied, "Actually, no. That was the moment I asked Jesus Christ into my life." The Twins may have worked hard to win the pennant, but Greg Gagne was given salvation free for asking by faith!

Two Old Testament characters demonstrate that God's method of justifying (saving) men has always been by faith in His promised Messiah. This faith is totally apart from human works. Genesis 15:6 says that Abraham, the spiritual father of Jews and Christians, did nothing but believe God's promise to be justified. If Abraham had been saved from his sin by his own good deeds, he could have boasted before men — but not before a perfect God! But salvation is a free gift. It is not a reward for our righteousness, for we have none! God declares wicked men (that's us) to be righteous when we simply trust Jesus (God's Promised One). The only kind of men who are saved are the wicked who admit their condition! What a paradox! Anyone who thinks he can do any good thing to help save himself is not saved!

Faith is not man's action. It trusts the actions of someone else — Jesus Christ! Faith is not a ritual like circumcision, baptism or communion. These are signs to identify believers. Abraham was saved for at least 13 years before

God told him to be circumcised. Saving faith *results* in action (dynamic service). These good works are signs which justify man before other men (Names 2:14-26). Men are justified before a holy God by faith alone! *God* saves men by grace through faith. *We* recognize the saved ones by their deeds (Matthew 7:16).

King David sinned grievously by committing adultery and murder. In Psalm 51, he confessed by labeling his actions sin ("missing the mark"), transgressions ("overstepping the line") and iniquity ("inborn tendency to sin and transgress"). Though David suffered God's chastening and had great sorrow, he was forgiven apart from any of his works. The work of Jesus on the cross provided his salvation. What was free to David was very costly to Jesus!

Furthermore, it was not by keeping the Law that Abraham or anyone else was saved (v. 13). The Law was given 430 years after Abraham was justified (Galatians 3:17-18)! Abraham, our spiritual "father," was saved by faith in God's promised Savior, just as we are. This faith "counted" as righteousness when he had no righteousness. Jesus' resurrection guarantees the justification (salvation) of *all* who believe, whether in Abraham's or in our day. The glory belongs to God, so we can never boast. What a gift! What a God!

The Results of Being Justified

Therefore, since we have been justified through faith, we have peace with God through our Lord Jesus Christ . . .

Romans 5:1

AMERICANS HAVE NO PROBLEM looking for results. We are so pragmatic. We want to immediately know the outcome. We want to check the scorecard of our games! Who won or lost is more important to most of us than the hows or the whys.

God is concerned about results as well, though He is also concerned with the hows and the whys. When it comes to our salvation (justification), we are saved *by* grace through faith so that we might bring glory to Him. That is how and why we were saved.

All believers in Jesus are justified. Justification indicates a "one-time, legal declaration with continuing results." Romans 5:1-5 lists at least five major results of being justified before God.

First, we have peace with God. This is not a temporary armistice or truce, but a permanent erasure of all enmity. Before being saved, we were at war with God. We were His enemies (James 4:4; Colossians 1:21). We were under His wrath. We were rebellious criminals when He sought us out. We weren't even looking for God. We were empty when He filled us. Ephesians 2:14 says that Jesus Christ Himself *is* our peace. Colossians 1:20 says He made peace by the blood of His cross. What could be more valuable? Peace with God is an objective reality, not a subjective feeling. God gave us a relationship *with* Himself the instant we believed upon Jesus. Now it is possible to enjoy the peace *of* God as we obey Him (Philippians 4:7). But only by obeying Him daily will we enjoy the peace He has given!

Second, we have access into His grace in the royal courtroom of heaven. We may go directly to God in prayer

27

through our Lord Jesus Christ. Access means "a way in." Jesus is the Door (John 10:9). He is the Way (John 14:6). We are not on the outside looking in. If you tried to call the President of the United States, you could not talk to him. To the unbeliever, God is as unavailable as the President! But Jesus Christ gives the believer immediate access to God. He is our Mediation!

Third, we have the hope of His glory. We will see Him some day in all His glory! This hope has no element of uncertainty, as when we say, "I hope to get four hits today." The New Testament word for "hope" means a "certain reality." It means salvation is a "done deal." Only a believer can rejoice in his future!

Fourth, we can rejoice when suffering through the inevitable troubles that come because of our relationship to Jesus. He suffered in this world and we are not above our Master. This suffering produces *proven* character and more hope as the Holy Spirit encourages us. The indwelling Holy Spirit, given at the moment we believed, keeps us from crumbling under the weight of trials. These trials, sent by God for our growth and fruitfulness, develop us spiritually. We should welcome them as friends (James 1:2-4).

Fifth, God "pours out His love" into our hearts like a flood. It remains permanently! The Holy Spirit gives us a sense that a personal God, not "somebody up there," loves us. We have God's love with which to love Him and others (1 John 3-4)!

Justification makes us winners in Christ. That's what God's scorecard says! What great results for the children of God!

A Line Drive

But God demonstrates his own love for us in this: While we were still sinners, Christ died for us.

Romans 5:8

BASEBALL COACHES TEACH hitters to hit line drives. The odds of a hit are far greater if the ball is a line drive rather than if it is a high fly or a grounder. Many years ago, a promising Cleveland Indian lefthander named Herb Score was hit in the head by a line drive off the bat of the Yankees' Gil McDougald. He was never as effective again. In 1962, the Giants Willie McCovey hit a line drive at Yankee second baseman Bobby Richardson. It was the ninth inning of the seventh game of the World Series, the Yanks led by a run and the bases were loaded with two out. Bobby caught the ball to end the game and give New York the Series. Two line drives resulted in two different outcomes.

God has hit a "line drive" right at each one of us. It is this: "While we were still sinners, Christ died for us." If we will receive His love and forgiveness, we will experience joy, victory, and eternal life. But if we refuse to receive Jesus Christ as Savior, God's line drive will hit us! Eternal death (separation from God) in the lake of fire will be our choice, as we pay the consequences for our unbelief.

Jesus died for ungodly sinners at just the right time, the time God chose (v. 5). There was no merit in us that would compel Him to give His life. He died for us because God loved us in spite of ourselves! But God didn't save us by His love. He saved us by grace (Ephesians 2:8-9). God was not taken by surprise by our disobedience but He cannot just slip us into heaven because He loves us, or He would be no better than a crooked judge who lets a criminal off. He *planned* Jesus' redemptive death to pay for our sins before He even created us (Ephesians 1:4)! How amazing that the perfect Son of God would die for ungodly sinners!

29

Jesus Christ is the "capstone," rejected by the builders of religious systems (Matthew 21:42-46). But He is the center of a real relationship to God. If you will fall upon Him for mercy, you will be broken as you realize your sinfulness. But if He falls upon you in judgment, you will be crushed forever without hope. You must catch His "line drive" before it hits you!

Reconciliation

For if (since) when we were God's enemies, we were recon-
ciled to him through the death of his Son, how much more,
having been reconciled, shall we be saved through his life!
Romans 5:10

A JUDGE HAD a much loved son who stole a large sum of money and fled the country. By his deed, the son established an estranged relationship between himself and his father. The father still loved the son, but now he had to view him as a lawbreaker. He was obligated to put a price upon the head of the son. If the son ever returned to the jurisdiction of the court, the father was bound to try, sentence and punish him.

But while the son was a fugitive from justice, the father's compassion caused him to sacrifice all his property to repay everything the son had stolen. The father and the law were reconciled to the son. They can now receive the son back without sending him to prison. The son may come back or he may not, but the only thing standing in his way is his own will.

Dr. Robert Moyer used the above illustration to explain how God has reconciled rebellious man. We have rebelled against God and heaven and broken God's laws. A righteous God had to put a price on our heads. But God became incarnate in Jesus Christ and paid the debt at the cross. God did not change. He has always loved us. Neither did the transaction change the world, for most of mankind remains in rebellion against God. But God no longer has to punish those who come to Him, as criminals! He is reconciled. We can be reconciled if we will only believe and receive His free gift!

Jesus died for all, but *instead* of only those who will receive Him! Paul writes that we (believers) are saved from God's wrath. During the Great Tribulation Period, spoken

31

of by Zephaniah and other prophets, God will pour out this wrath upon rebellious mankind. But believers in Jesus will be removed first (1 Thessalonians 5:9).

Believers in Jesus Christ are eternally secure, for Jesus died to save us and He lives today to keep us saved (v. 10). He constantly intercedes for us in heaven (Hebrews 7:25). We will never be condemned to hell (Romans 8:1).

What joy for all who believe and receive the Lord Jesus Christ! No matter what happens to us on earth, we rejoice because we are saved from wrath and kept saved by Jesus Christ.

Adam's Fumble
and Christ's Recovery

For if, by the trespass of the one man, death reigned through that one man, how much more will those who receive God's abundant provision of grace and of the gift of righteousness reign in life through the one man, Jesus Christ.

Romans 5:17

SOME NFL RUNNING BACKS are great runners, but have a tendency to fumble. We sometimes look at their yards gained and wonder why they don't play more. But when we compare carries with turnovers, it becomes evident they fumble too often.

The first man, Adam, "fumbled the ball" when he sinned in the Garden of Eden (Genesis 2 and 3). His sin of disobedience brought death ("separation") to all of us, his offspring. This death is spiritual, physical, and eternal. Spiritual death is separation from God. Physical death is separation of body from soul and spirit. Eternal death, or the "second death" (Revelation 20:6, 14), is forever being separated from God and it involves torment in the lake of fire. All who leave this world without receiving Jesus' death on their behalf suffer eternal death.

As Author of nature, God has decreed a natural law that man begets offspring like himself. When Adam sinned, the inborn propensity to sin entered the entire human race. The inherent sinful nature has been passed on to every descendent, including you and me. Adam "sinned away" the rulership over God's creation. Death took over. The proof of this is that death reigned from Adam to Moses (v. 14), before any law was given! Even infants and the insane all died because the received a dying nature from Adam. "In Adam" all of us die, for we are sinners from the moment of conception (Psalm 51:5). We sin because we are sinners. It is our nature to sin.

The action of both Adam and Jesus Christ affected many others. One sin of disobedience by Adam meant condemnation for all men (v. 18). But one obedient act of righteousness (Jesus' sacrifice on the cross) means life for all who receive Him! We can spiritually and eternally be "born again!" This salvation is offered to all!

God added the Law of Moses so we might *see* how evil we are (v. 20). It reveals that *all* of us fall short. Sin is universal. Everyone either remains in Adam's race and under condemnation or he becomes "born again" into Christ's race and is forgiven and justified. Only by seeing our sin do we see how much *grace* it took for Christ to save us.

Christ has recovered Adam's fumble, but we gain much more "in Christ" than Adam lost. Why did God allow sin in the first place? He wants our free will worship. We are now heirs of God. We have a heavenly home. We will be with Christ forever and we will be like Him. All this comes through faith in the redemption that is in Christ Jesus! What a Savior!

Dead Men Walking

For we know that our old self was crucified with him . . .
count yourselves dead to sin, but alive to God in Christ Jesus
. . . Offer yourselves to God . . .

Romans 6:6, 11, 13

DURING THE 1860s, a man named Wyatt was called to
fight for the South in the Civil War. Because of his many
responsibilities, another young man, Pratt by name, offered to go in his place. Pratt went into battle bearing the
name and number of Wyatt. Soon, Pratt was killed in action. Since he was the substitute of the other man, it was
legally recorded that Wyatt was killed. Sometime later,
Wyatt was called for service in the army, but he calmly
told recruiters that he had been killed in action. The records
were checked and, though he stood before them, he was
dead in the eyes of the law! He had died in the person of
his substitute!

The Pratt/Wyatt substitution helps us to understand
what happened when our old nature died in Jesus Christ
at the cross 2,000 years ago. Sin is ugly. It brought only
death. There is nothing good about it, no matter how glit-
tering Satan makes it seem. When we received Jesus Christ
as Savior, we confessed ourselves to be sinners and worthy of death. We died to sin (past tense) when we were
saved. Death, however, means separation, not extinction.
We cannot *live* in sin if we have *died* to sin!

The symbol of water baptism pictures the death of our
old selfish nature and our resurrection up out of the water in the power of God's Spirit. This is the same power
that raised Jesus from the dead! That is the theme of chapters 6, 7, and 8 of Romans.

As "dead men walking," we have three orders in chapter 6. First, we are to *know* the truth of our death in Jesus.
We were declared righteous ("justified") when we believed

upon Jesus. The guilt and penalty of sin was removed. But now God wants to make us righteous in practice, removing the growth and power of sin. This is what it means to be sanctified ("set apart"). Sanctification is what changes us to resemble Jesus, a process that never ends while we are in this body. We must know our old nature is crucified and we need not yield to it. We are grafted into Jesus as a branch is grafted into a tree. His life is now our life.

Second, we must reckon (count) upon our death and upon Christ's life in us. Our old nature is powerless to control our actions when we count it dead. Sometimes, it is wiggling and twisting on the cross, protesting it's demise. "Me first," "Have it your way," "Do what comes naturally," "Look out for No. 1," "self-gratification now," it screams! Are you tempted to be jealous? Are you sensitive to criticism? Reckon yourself dead. Dead men can't be offended. Are you over inflated by praise? Remember, you are dead. Only God's opinion matters!

Third, we must offer our bodies to God. Augustine knew this truth. One day, he met a woman who had been his mistress before he was saved. She wanted to have sex with him again. He quickly turned and walked away. She called out, "Augustine, it's me! It's me!" Over his shoulder, he called back, "Yes, I know, but it's no longer me!"

Galatians 2:20 says we were crucified when Christ was crucified. God, through evil men, put Jesus on the cross and us with Him. We could not crucify ourselves. He did it to destroy sin in us. Crucifixion can be a slow, painful death. It sometimes takes believers a while to *know* they are dead, to *reckon* upon it, and to *present* their bodies to God. Paul does not say we never sin anymore, but he does say we can never live in sin as a way of life. The sooner we know, reckon and present, the less the agony, for dead men no longer feel the pain!

Two Leaders

But now that you have been set free from sin and have become slaves to God, the benefit you reap leads to holiness and the result is eternal life.

Romans 6:22

EVERY ONE OF US has great potential to lead those who respect us. Sports stars are not exceptions. A celebrity hero may drink alcohol, father children out of wedlock, and break the law, but such a person is an unworthy hero. He should not be followed. Another type of hero is one who walks with God and becomes humble, gracious, and dependable. This type of leader contributes to society. Such a leader is worthy to be followed.

Some people (Antinomians) had the idea that since we are saved and kept saved by grace, they could live any way they pleased! So, Paul discussed the two leaders to which humans submit. He knew we all serve someone or something and there is no middle ground or no gray area.

The first leader in our conduct is sin. Sin is progressive. It leads to further impurity and ever-increasing wickedness, produces shame, and pays off in death. Sin is like a vicious animal whose appetite only increases when it is fed. It results in slavery. The only freedom known by a person ruled by sin is freedom from righteousness. The "wages" of sin is death.

Another leader of mankind is God, and He produces righteousness. The righteousness of God leads to holiness ("separation from sin"). The result of God's righteousness is the free *gift* of eternal life! A true believer in Jesus is saved by grace and he does not habitually and continually sin (6:1-2). Neither does he want to sin occasionally (6:15). These verses are Paul's reply to antinomianism.

God sets a clear choice before all men (Deuteronomy 30:19). One choice is to follow sin and to receive death. We can choose to remain hopelessly lost, separated from God, and to suffer in hell for eternity. Or, we can choose reconciliation to a loving God and all the joys of life forever with Him. No man can serve two masters (Matthew 6:24). God wants us to choose life!

Marriage and Professional Players

So, my brothers, you died to the law through the body of Christ, that you might belong to another, to him who was raised from the dead, in order that we might bear fruit to God.

Romans 7:4

MARRIAGES ARE BINDING in God's eyes. So are contracts that players sign with professional teams. A woman who marries a man is bound to him until the death of that man. A player who signs a pro contract is no longer an amateur and is not eligible to compete on the college level. He becomes united to his pro team. A woman may re-marry when her husband dies. Likewise, a player may play for a pro team only when he "dies" to his amateur status.

What do marriages and pro players have to do with Christians? They illustrate our "death" to the law. The law of God is good, but before He gave His law to man the knowledge of the depth of our sinful nature was dormant. God's law revealed the dreadful nature and desperate power of sin. It is a "mirror" revealing our dirty minds and deceitful hearts. Most people like to look into a mirror — except the mirror of God's Word!

Sin is a violation of God's law. The more law we know and try to keep, the more we realize our sin. The law spells death to our best hopes of earning heaven or of living a holy life by our own efforts. A person who is not born again (saved) has only a sinful nature which can do no good in God's eyes. When one becomes born again (saved), God gives us a new nature. It's purpose is to produce fruit for God. We can do good through His power, for we become His "workmanship" (Ephesians 2:10). When Christ died at Calvary, God considered us dead to the law (v. 4). We became free from law-keeping as a way of earning salvation or living righteously! We are now "married" to Christ.

We have "signed" a "pro contract."

But now we have an internal battle! The old nature, which can do no good, wages war against our new nature, which can't sin (1 John 3:9)! The apostle Paul became very introspective in Romans 7:9-25. He used a personal pronoun 50 times to describe his own present, daily conflict with indwelling sin! You might say he had an overdose of Vitamin "I." But victory over sin could not be found within him, for there is no power even in the new nature! Only the Holy Spirit's power can energize our new natures (Romans 8). Paul did not understand his weak sin nature (v. 15). Nor can we. Sin is subtle (v. 8), ugly (v. 13), dominating (v. 17), and aggressive (v. 23). We are saved from sin's guilt and penalty and when Jesus comes we will be saved from sin's presence. Until then, we must rely upon the power of the Holy Spirit every day. All our own good intentions end in failure.

Tradition says an ancient tribe near Tarsus (Paul's home) tied the body of a murder victim to the murderer, slowly allowing the decaying corpse to infect and execute the murderer. We must be delivered ("as a soldier pulls a wounded comrade from the battlefield") from this "body of death" (the "sin principle" within). This is done when we reckon ourselves crucified with Christ and dead to sin and law (Galatians 2:20).

God hates anything we try to accomplish in our selfish nature. He will not use it (John 3:16). Some believers still try to live by the law in the power of their old nature. How ridiculous! The Christian life is Christ living through us! We are "married" to Jesus Christ! The "contract" is signed in His blood and we are no longer amateurs.

"Sic 'em, Spirit"

You, however, are controlled not by the sinful nature but by the Spirit, if (since) the Spirit of God lives in you. And if anyone does not have the Spirit of Christ, he does not belong to Christ.

Romans 8:9

H. A. IRONSIDE TOLD the story of an American Indian who was telling his tribe of his Christian conversion. He told how in the beginning he felt he would never sin again. He was so happy. But, as time went by, he recognized an inward conflict.

"It seems, my brothers, that I have two dogs fighting in my heart: One is a very good dog, a beautiful white dog, and he is always watching out for my best interests. The other is a very bad dog, a black dog, who is always trying to destroy the things that I want to see built up. These dogs give me a lot of trouble because they are always quarreling and fighting with each other."

"Which one wins?" asked a listener.

"Which ever one I say 'sic 'em to," replied the Indian.

The apostle Paul revealed his frustrating struggle with sin (Chapter 6) and law-keeping (Chapter 7). But in Chapter 8, he revealed the power to live righteously. The Holy Spirit, who indwells all believers, *provides great victory over sin and our old nature!* All we need to do is say, "Sic, 'em," letting Him have His way! The law (principle) of life overcomes the law (principle) of death just as the principle of flight overcomes the principle of gravity. The power comes from the Spirit of God!

Paul begins this chapter by saying that there is no condemnation to those in Christ Jesus. We are eternally saved! We are not on probation to see if we merit heaven! The infinite price of our salvation was paid by the infinite One!

But all of us still have an old sin nature. This principle (law) of sin and the death that results wages constant war

41

against the principle (law) of the indwelling Spirit and our new life. We can't fight in our own strength, but the Holy Spirit (mentioned 20 times in chapter 8) battles for us. He *manifests our new life* when we relinquish control to Him! *He is the secret to enjoying life.* In fact, *He is the Christian life!* Just as He raised Jesus from the dead, *He will resurrect us* because *He indwells us.* Believers in Jesus are *defined* as those who walk (live) according to the Spirit and not according to their sin nature (vs. 4, 14). The presence of salvation is determined by the presence of the Holy Spirit. We receive all of the Holy Spirit the moment we believe in Jesus, but He gets more of us day by day! Unredeemed man has no inclination or power to please God (vs. 5-8). Man cares only for his selfish interests. Natural man may have religion, morality, sincerity, zeal, sacrifice, suffering, philanthropy, or church membership, but God is not impressed. These outward acts may come from a heart that is by nature in rebellion. The estrangement between holy God and sinful man is mutual. Only *death* to the old nature and life provided by the Spirit can please God. There is no relationship to Christ apart from the Spirit. God doesn't want the dedication of the old sinful nature. He wants our trust in His Spirit to do what we cannot do — live for Christ.

We owe nothing to the old nature (flesh). If it had its way, it would drag us down to the deepest, darkest, hottest place in hell! We rightly care for our bodies, but care for these bodies should make us hate both sin and the sinful nature, for sin is the cause of the death of these wonderful bodies! Why be obligated to such an enemy? Christ is the One who saved us and *His Spirit fills and keeps us.*

God's Spirit leads (not drives) Christians. A person who habitually lives in his old sinful nature is not saved in the first place (v. 13), for God's Spirit is so real *He makes His presence known* in every believer! To be led by God's Spirit means we desire to please God. We are concerned about eternal values such as the souls of others and our future rewards in Heaven. God's Spirit *assures us we are God's children.* By His Spirit we cry out "Abba" ("Daddy") to our loving Heavenly Father. Our relationship to God is *tender and free of anxiety* because of the Holy Spirit. We are "joint-heirs" (not "part-heirs") with Jesus Christ in all He attained by His death and resurrection (v. 17)! What wonderful benefits He provides! Suffering the reproach of this non-believing world is automatically part of our lives, but we have a great future! *It's a future guaranteed by the Holy Spirit.* "Sic 'em, Spirit!"

Eager Expectation

*The creation waits in eager expectation for the sons of God
to be revealed.*

Romans 8:19

REMEMBER AS A KID the eager expectation of your first
ball game of the new season? You barely slept the night
before. Just putting on the uniform made you so excited!
As your parents drove you to the field, you couldn't sit
still in the back seat because of the excitement! Something great was about to happen!

Something great is about to happen to this world, too.
But it is still future. Robert Browning wrote, "God is in His
Heaven — all's right with the world." But that statement
is not true. God is in Heaven all right, but something is
terribly wrong with this world. He has judged sin with an
awful curse on the earth. When Adam disobeyed Him, God
cursed the entire creation (Genesis 3). It was immediately
subjected to frustration (futility, frailty, and purposelessness). Decay set in by God's decree. Adam died spiritually
and eventually he died physically. Sickness, pain, and
suffering resulted. Weeds and thorns grew. Barren deserts
replaced lush vegetation. Animals became carnivorous as
the "law of the jungle" prevailed. Floods, earthquakes, and
drought rocked the planet. Creation is nowhere near its
original condition — or its final conclusion.

Every person born is born spiritually dead because we
are Adam's offspring. From the moment of birth we begin
to die physically. We cannot escape the sufferings of the
present, though we have more comforts than any previous generation. But one day, the curse will be removed!
Because of Jesus' atonement for sin, all who believe in
Him will be redeemed and given healthy new bodies! We
will live on a new earth that is free from sin and its effects!
Creation groans outwardly and Christians groan inwardly
as we eagerly anticipate that day! With the expectation of

44

such a future glory, our present suffering is called "light" and "momentary" (2 Corinthians 4:17).

Meanwhile, the Holy Spirit groans too! Given to all believers in Jesus, the Holy Spirit is the "first fruits" or "down payment" on the glory awaiting us! He assures us that we have eternal life because we are "in Christ." Sometimes we don't know how to pray because we don't know God's will. The Holy Spirit prays for us with an inaudible groan. He always knows God's will! In this sense, a groan is the most spiritual prayer! It is not our eloquence that causes God to act, but the Sprit's groanings in intercession for us. Prayer is not the means of getting what we want. It is the means for God to get what He wants! He puts the prayer into our hearts. No wonder we must not grieve (Ephesians 4:30) or quench (1 Thessalonians 5:19) the Holy Spirit! He's our hope! He's our motivational power! He's why we have "eager expectation" of a wonderful future!

His Followers Can't Lose!

And we know that in all things God works for the good of those who love him, who have been called according to his purpose.

Romans 8:28

CHRISTIANS DON'T HAVE TO RELY on superstition. We have something better — the Providence of God. Romans 8:28 is the pinnacle of the book of Romans, for it reveals that God uses everything that happens — even suffering — for our eternal benefit in line with His eternal purpose! What is His purpose for us? He has determined that we are to be like Jesus! God's providence means He orchestrates everything that happens. His Sovereignty means He causes or allows everything that happens. He is not to blame for sin or evil, but He supernaturally uses them to accomplish an ultimate purpose. What an awesome God! We must thank Him *in* all things as well as *for* all things (1 Thessalonians 5:18; Philippians 4:6). (?)

God led Israel through the desert for a purpose (Deuteronomy 8:15-16). He led Joseph through suffering to glory and Joseph said, "God meant it for good (Genesis 50:20). Job said, "Though he slay me, yet will I hope in him" (Job 13:15). Romans 8:28 is more than a promise. It is an unchangeable fact. It is best learned via adversity. In "all" (not "most") things, God works to make us just like His Son, Jesus Christ! Chance, luck, or fate have nothing to do with us. Stepping on lines, crossing bats, or uncrossing them have no effect. Things do not just happen to a believer in Jesus. There are no accidents in a Christian's life — only incidents designed by God for our good and His glory. Those outside of Christ have no such promise.

Why are we so sure God works everything out for good? First, because He says so! That is reason enough. Paul says, "we know" not "we feel like" God works out all for

46

our good. Often we don't *feel* like it. It is better to *know* it! Second, He *"foreknew"* us before birth. He gave us the grace to say "yes" to Jesus. Yet, He does not manipulate us like puppets. Our limited minds cannot fully grasp this concept. Furthermore, He *predestined* ("marked out or determined beforehand) us to be just like Jesus some day. We will be free from all sin! Predestination is true of all believers. We will have new bodies (1 Corinthians 15:35-58). What eternal security He gives us!

God has also *called* ("elected") us to salvation. He chose us (John 15:16, 19) before we were born or the earth was created (Ephesians 1:4). Yet, all men are responsible and have a free will. These two truths are like the two sides of a roof that meet above the clouds. We know they meet, but we cannot see them meet! Henry Ward Beecher said that the elect are those "whosoever will" believe in Jesus Christ and the non-elect are those "whosoever won't" believe in Him. This eliminates all pride, presumption, and despair for the Christian.

God *justified* all those He called. He views us as just! Justification is not "because of" our faith, but "by faith" He gives us the faith to believe (Ephesians 2:8-9).He *glorified* those He justified. Scripture speaks of our glorification as though it already happened. Paul used past tense for a future event to stress the present reality of our glorification! It is future but it is sure!

God, not men or women, does all these things. He cannot lie or fail. The Good Shepherd who saved 100 sheep will take all 100 sheep to heaven. Not one of God's sheep will ever be lost. In the turmoil of the present, nothing could be of greater encouragement than to know these truths. Believers in Jesus can not lose and we need not rely on superstition or myth!

Super Winners

Who will bring any charge against those whom God has chosen? It is God who justifies.

Romans 8:33

AS A CHILD, Phyllis Egan dreaded "choose-up" games. She hated the prospect of being the last one chosen, or of not being chosen at all!

"When I received Jesus Christ as Savior and read that He had chosen me, it changed my entire self-concept," she said. "I said, 'Yes!' Somebody picked me! Jesus really does want me! God is for me!"

The more we learn about most things, the less we stand in awe of them. But the more we learn about the wonderful mysteries of our salvation, the more we admire and appreciate the Lord Jesus Christ! He chose us and He is for us! It doesn't matter who opposes believers in Jesus. God is for us. He gave us His Son when we were lost sinners and enemies of God. He spared Abraham's son (Genesis 22) but not His own Son! Now that we are His children, He won't give us less than He gave us when we were enemies! He will give us the fulfillment of all His promises, too!

We are His elect ("called") ones. It doesn't matter who would condemn ("press charges against") or criticize us. God justifies us! He sees me just-as-if-I'd never sinned. Satan accuses us (Revelation 12:10) and he is correct. We are sinners. But his charges are "thrown out of court" because Jesus died for us! Then He arose from the dead and returned to heaven to intercede (pray) for us before the Father!

Woodrow Kroll writes, "By His victorious death, His victorious resurrection, His victorious ascension into heaven and His victorious intercession for us, the Lord Jesus has sealed the eternal purpose of God." You may forget to pray for yourself, but Jesus doesn't forget. He is seated at the right hand (the "power position") of God, making intercession for you.

Paul knew by experience (not just theory) that nothing could separate the believer from God's love. He wrote his

48

own autobiography (and that of many Christian martyrs) in verses 35-36. This world has always hated true Christians. The early Christians were considered nothing more than defenseless animals to be slaughtered. But we win because nothing can undo the finished work of Christ completed on the cross. We are more than conquerors (hypernikaō = "superconquerors") through Him (not through ourselves).

Death or fear of death cannot separate us from Him. Many Christian martyrs have thanked their murderers for sending them to Jesus. The enemy has sometimes been baffled and overcome by their invincible courage.

The trials, temptation, disappointments, failings, and uncertainties of life, though often harder than death, cannot separate us from God's love.

Angels cannot separate us from Him. The fallen ones (demons) are restrained enemies and the good ones are engaged friends!

Neither miracles or people in positions of authority (powers) can separate us. Nor can present circumstances or future problems separate us from Jesus. Both are interwoven with His favor. We have eternal security. Like gold in fire, we lose only the dross and our reward is very great!

"Height" and "depth" are common astronomical terms used to trace the high and low points of a star's path. All of space from top to bottom cannot separate us from God's love. Neither can the height of prosperity nor the depth of poverty. Nothing can swoop down from above or creep up from below to separate us from God. Satan, self, and evil men are insufficient to destroy us!

"An old song says it quite well:

> Blessed assurance, Jesus is mine.
> O what a foretaste of glory divine.
> Heir of salvation, purchase of God,
> Born of His Spirit, washed in His blood.
> This is my story, this is my song:
> Praising my Savior all the day long."

Vernon McGee says, "We entered this chapter (8) with 'no condemnation,' we conclude it with 'no separation,' and in between 'all things work together for good.'" You just can't improve upon this!

God's Sovereign Choice

Therefore, God has mercy on whom he wants to have mercy, and he hardens whom he wants to harden.

Romans 9:18

PRO SPORTS TEAMS CONDUCT DRAFTS to spread talent among themselves. In baseball, football, and basketball, each team takes its turn selecting athletes for the future. The athlete must sign with their team or wait until the next draft. The organization makes the sovereign choice, but the athlete is responsible to sign on the dotted line.

Chapter 9 begins the most difficult section of Romans. It outlines the sovereign choice of God in selecting (electing) the nation of Israel for great blessing. The topic is God's Sovereignty and man's responsibility. We accept by faith that both are true. They are like the two sides of a roof. The peak meets in the clouds above our heads, so our finite minds cannot entirely comprehend all about each truth. Let's examine them anyway!

Paul was accused of being an enemy of Israel. But he was a devoted Jewish man who loved his nation dearly. He had constant anguish in his heart because his people rejected the Messiah. If it were possible (and it was not), Paul was willing to be separated from Jesus if it meant Israel's salvation. His attitude resembles that of Moses (Exodus 32:31-32). It, too, is very hard to understand.

God chose Israel. Man has a free will. Israel as a nation (not every Israelite) will one day be saved. He will step in before she totally destroys herself. He deserves praise that any Jew or Gentile is saved at all! His truth offends our human reasoning, for Israel surely did not deserve to be chosen. We must subordinate our reasoning to faith in God and His Word. Israel was adopted as God's Son. He revealed His glory to Israel, made covenants (agreements) with Israel, gave the law to Israel, and explained to them how to worship. God promised Israel blessings when they

50

are in their land of Palestine worshipping the Messiah, Jesus Christ. God gave Israel Abraham, Isaac, and Jacob, and ultimately Jesus came through Israel.

Though thousands of Jews have believed in Jesus Christ, the nation has failed to do so (vs. 6-10). It has been temporarily set aside. Jewish rabbis taught that circumcision meant one was God's child, but Paul said that was not true (v. 6). Grace does not run in physical bloodlines. Grace is available only in the blood of Jesus!

In verses 11-13, God's election relates to earthly privilege and not eternal destiny. Jacob was loved and Esau "hated." "Hated" is a relative term indicating God's favor of Israel over other nations. The quote is from Malachi, written 2,000 years after the men lived. Two nations had come from them.

God is morally right in everything He does (v. 14). He is governor of His universe and He can use whomever He wishes. He operates upon the just principle of His eternal purpose. For example, God hardened Pharaoh's heart after Pharaoh hardened his own heart (Exodus 5:2, 7:3, 13). You might say Pharaoh chose to allow cement into his heart and God allowed it to dry (Exodus 5:21, 7:23, 9:12, 10:1, 20:27, 11:10, 14:4, 8)!

God is not answerable to man. The Creator is greater than the creation. We do not have His wisdom. All of us are clay in the Potter"s hand and He can make each of us for different purposes. Jews who sought righteousness based upon works didn't find it. They stumbled over Jesus. Non-Jews who realized their spiritual bankruptcy and sought righteousness by faith found it!

A number of Old Testament prophecies reveal God's principle of election (Hosea 2:23). But it is still "over our heads." You can be saved if you want to. Simply believe in Jesus. If you do so, you are one of God's elect. If you refuse to do so, you are not!

Enthusiastically Wrong

For I can testify about them that they are zealous for God but their zeal is not based on knowledge.

Romans 10:2

BASEBALL PLAYERS are notoriously and enthusiastically superstitious. Babe Ruth always stepped on second base on his way in from the outfield and Willie Mays always kicked it. Lefty O'Doul, a Yankee pitcher in the 20s said, "It's not that if I stepped on the foul line it would really lose the game, but why take a chance?" These men and others have their superstitions with enthusiastic error!

Those who confuse the two different kinds of righteousness become satisfied with their own righteousness, even though they are dying of a fatal disease. They resemble a woman who uses a lot of makeup to look good externally while she is dying of cancer internally. Secondly, they look down on others because they have no absolute standard by which to judge themselves. They resent Jesus and the gospel because they cannot come up to His standard. That's why He was (and is) so hated. They misuse God's law. Finally, they fail to submit to God's standard and seek Christ.

As a nation, Israel rejected God's message of redemption in Jesus Christ. When she did so, she enthusiastically and wrongly sought to become righteous in her own way. Israel became passionately devoted to law. The religious leaders read and memorized God's law, but never internalized the truth. The law said, "Do this and you will live." But man cannot keep the law! Jesus came and said, "Believe on me and live." He fulfilled the law and is the only righteous One. The law can make no one righteous. It was given to show us our unrighteousness. Sadly, the Jews rebelled against God and rejected the only Savior, even though He was near to them! They were passionate, but blind and misguided. They could do nothing to bring

Christ down and earn salvation. They must not seek signs, wonders, or new revelation. We have the gospel, which is all we need to be saved!

All Israel or anyone else must do to be saved ("rescued from destruction") is confess "Jesus is Lord." This phrase is crammed with meaning. It means Jesus is 100 percent God. It means Jesus' work is 100 percent sufficient to save us. It means Jesus has 100 percent right to rule our lives. Everyone (Jew or Gentile) who does this will be saved (v. 13). What a great promise! Those who believe Him in their hearts will confess Him before others in word and deed (Matthew 10:32-33).

Preachers are needed to spread this good news about belief in Jesus, for faith comes by hearing God's Word (v. 17). Paul was a preacher, and he prayed for the salvation of unbelieving Jews even though they became his most bitter enemies.

By nature, all of us are deceitful and wicked (Jeremiah 17:9). We are children of wrath (Ephesians 2:3). We try to establish our own righteousness but fail. Men's philosophies vary from, "do the best you can," to "you'll be saved if good deeds outweigh bad ones," to "at least I'm better than my neighbor." All of these fall short of God's standard for heaven. We may be sincere, but totally wrong! By nature, we can no more be righteous than we can change our skin color!

Romans 9 was about God's election of us to salvation. Romans 10 is about our responsibility. Both are true.

Whose report about man's condition will you believe (v. 16)? Man claims to be righteous. God says we are lost sinners apart from Jesus Christ. We must trust Jesus to be saved. Will you believe man and perish or will you believe God and live?

The Plan

Oh, the depth of the riches of the wisdom and knowledge of God! How unsearchable his judgments, and his paths beyond tracing out!

Who has known the mind of the Lord? Or who has been his counselor?

Who has ever given to God that God should repay him? For from him and through him and to him are all things. To him be the glory forever! Amen.

Romans 11:33-36

ROGER MASON was a major league pitcher during the 80s and 90s. One day, he was reading a prophecy book. On the last page was a suggested prayer that told how to accept Christ. Roger says, "I did it, and my life has never been the same." A writer later approached him at a Triple A All-Star Game in Louisville. "This is God's career," Roger told the writer. "He has reasons for sending me here even though I don't understand it.'" Roger knew God had a plan for his life.

God has a plan for His world. His plan will come to pass. We do not always understand all the details of God's plan because we are not all-knowing like God is. We cannot figure out by our own reasoning power. Furthermore, He didn't ask us what He should do when He devised His eternal plan! He owes us no explanations, for He is God and we are but man. He alone is sovereign. His sovereignty means He causes or allows all things to happen that do happen and He prevents other things from happening. We simply must turn our arguments with God into adoration of God, follow Him by faith, and give Him glory.

Romans 11 outlines part of God's plan for His world. Desiring that people love and serve Him, God unconditionally chose Israel to be His own people, to receive the revelation of Who God is, and to bring Jesus into the world.

In spite of His mercy to Israel, the nation rejected Him for their own "homemade" religion. God was not taken by surprise. He knew this would happen, though He did not cause it (James 1:13). He temporarily set Israel aside, "hardening" or "blinding" her with moral insensitivity. Today the nation Israel is in a stupor ("stinging caused by a poisonous bite") and insensitive to truth. She has temporarily lost privilege with God. Only a remnant of Jews believe Jesus and love Him. What God meant to be a blessing (salvation) became a trap (judgment) when Israel refused to believe God (v. 9). He is both kind to those who believe Him and stern to those who don't (v. 22).

Yet, the existence of Israel proves the truth of Scripture. God always has had a remnant of believing Jews like Paul. Elijah though he was the only believing Israelite left, but God said He had 7,000 faithful ones in hiding (1 Kings 19:18)! (Sometimes things are better than good men think!) Though God set Israel aside temporarily, He still saves individuals!

Paul says that Israel the nation lost privilege like a branch cut off from a tree. Now, God is calling non-Jews as a group (Acts 15:14). He has "grafted" Gentiles into the "tree" of His kingdom. He still saves individual Jews today, but is primarily saving Gentiles. When Israel comes to Christ, He will "graft" her back into the plan! That day is coming! Large numbers of Jews will receive Jesus Christ! When all Gentiles who will come to Christ do come (v. 25), God will resume dealing with Israel.

How merciful God is! He never changes His mind or His plan (Malachi 3:6; Hebrews 13:8). To appreciate God's mercy, we must see it against the dark background of our sin. Israel failed, yet God is merciful. Non-News are failing to fully embrace Christ. The church is full of apostasy, liberalism, moral failure, family breakdowns, and disrespect for God's Word. He will soon resume dealing with Israel. Even man's rebellion serves a purpose in His plan. What a plan! What a God!

Transformation

Therefore, I urge you, brothers, in view of God's mercy, to offer your bodies as living sacrifices, holy and pleasing to God — this is your spiritual act of worship. Do not conform any longer to the pattern of this world, but be transformed by the renewing of your mind. Then you will be able to test and approve what God's will is — his good, pleasing and perfect will.

Romans 12:1-2

IT IS ALWAYS GOD'S WAY to tell us who we are in Christ before encouraging us to live like we ought. He never asks us to live right so He can accept us. Romans is written to believers in Jesus Christ. Paul has told us of God's great mercy in chapters 1-11. He has called us "more than conquerors" through Him who loved us. He has just told us of God's great wisdom, knowledge, judgment, and glory. In view of these things, the Lord (through Paul) urges us to present our bodies to Him as living sacrifices. God could *demand* our allegiance. But He *asks* those He has saved to present our bodies as a way of worshipping Him. He is not asking us to earn or secure our salvation. He has saved our souls, the eternal part of us. He wants our bodies so He can express Himself through them to others.

He wants a living, not dead, sacrifice. He wants a holy ("devoted to the use of") sacrifice. Nothing less pleases Him. Dr. Arthur T. Pierson says,

> Suppose I owned a farm of 1000 acres. You come to me with the desire to purchase the farm. I agree, but upon one condition. I desire to retain one acre, right in the center of the farm, for my own use. Do you know that the law would permit me to build a road right across all the remainder of the farm, in order that I might have access to my one lone acre in the center of your land? Just so with the Chris-

56

tian who makes less than complete surrender to God. If he surrenders "999 acres" to God, retaining just one acre for himself, Satan will make a road right across the 999 acres, in order to reach the one unsurrendered part, and the whole life and service will be marred.

The world system has been set up by man to make himself happy without God. Satan is the god of the world, this age, and all who reject God's authority (2 Corinthians 4:4; John 12:31, 14:30, 16:11). This system has its own art, music, culture, religion, lifestyles and education. It wants our conformity and it hates non-conformists like Jesus Christ and His followers. Whoever loves this world becomes God's enemy! God says we should not let the world "press us into it's mold." Rather, we are to "be transformed" by the renewing of our minds. He transforms us daily (We can't do it) as we present our bodies to the Holy Spirit, and feed upon His Word and pray. God changes us every day! He causes us to think as He thinks about issues. He causes us to know His will, which is far better than our will. We are not to copy others, even those in church! We are to be transformed by God, renewed in the mind. Our life will be energized as we present ourselves to Him.

Have you presented your body today to the Holy Spirit?

Body Parts

Just as each one of us has one body with many members, and these members do not all have the same function, so in Christ we who are many form one body, and each member belongs to all the others.

Romans 12:4-5

MARIANO RIVERA is a tremendously talented closer for the New York Yankees. As such, he is an important part of the team. Yet, he is only one part, and he maintains a humble attitude.

"I don't believe in pride," he says. "I believe in the Lord. I believe when the kids see you, and they see that humble thing in you, they say, 'Wow, I want to be like him.' You just think natural. You're not going to be like, 'I'm the man!' You're a nobody! Always remember that the Lord has you there, whether you're a Christian or not. If it wasn't for the Lord, you wouldn't be there."

All believers are part of the "body" of Christ today. We are on His "team." He works through each of us. We are "in Him" and He is "in us" in the person of the Holy Spirit. Like Mariano Rivera, we must maintain a humble attitude as we realistically assess ourselves. No one has a monopoly on the Holy Spirit. We must not have a "superiority complex," nor should we envy others' parts on Christ's team. Pride is out. Our part is to be "crucified with Christ" (Galatians 2:20), yet walking around by faith in His resurrection power. We must not try to advance ourselves in Christian circles.

Each of us has a special gift ("charisma") from God. No gift is unnecessary, nor is it to be used for selfish reasons. We are to build others up with our gifts. Those who have the gift of prophecy or "inspired utterance" (1 Corinthians 14:1-5) are to use it in harmony with what has already been spoken by God in His Word.

Those who have the gift of serving ("diakonia") are to

use it to serve others. Those who have the gift of teaching ("making God's unchanging message understandable") must not neglect to teach. Teachers appeal to the mind, while exhorters appeal to the heart to encourage or console. Givers are to give generously and "with all their heart." Leaders must lead responsibly and diligently. Those who have a gift of showing mercy do practical deeds of kindness. They are to be cheerful and not sad.

An effective team uses the right person in the right position. An effective church does the same. When we all use our gifts correctly, an attitude of humility prevails. We recognize all gifts come from God and human pride is out. We serve the entire body and not the other way around!

Read Romans 12:9-21

Character Counts

Never be lacking in zeal, but keep your spiritual fervor, serving the Lord.

Romans 12:11

OREL HERSCHISER once told a reporter, "My greatest motivation for personal excellence is a willingness to submit myself to God and say, 'I'm going to be the best I can for You.'" Orel's character is a result of this willingness.

The apostle Paul was also a man of character and submission to God. Too, he was a very practical man. After describing our great need of salvation and God's wonderful provision in sending Christ to save us, he plainly outlines the character traits of God's followers. Without the power of the Holy Spirit, we cannot live to please God. But by His power we can love others. All deeds must flow out of this love.

Our love must be without hypocrisy. We must not be patting someone on the back with one hand and sticking a knife in his ribs with the other! We are to especially love other believers, honoring them above ourselves.

To love what is good means to hate evil. We must actually oppose evil in word and deed as we "stick like glue" to what is good (vs. 9-10). Jeremiah pronounced a curse on those who are lax in doing the Lord's work (Jeremiah 48:10). Our zeal ("diligence") must be maintained so that we are *always enthusiastic!* Being spiritually fervent means "boiling over" with commitment (v. 11). The only way to stay positive in a dark world is to look ahead with patient hope and to pray always (v. 12).

Giving to others in need and being hospitable wakes our minds off ourselves. So does blessing those who curse us. This is impossible without the power of the Holy Spirit. We are to be happy for other's success and sorrowful when they suffer. Empathy is a mark of greatness.

Pride precedes a fall. We are to live with humility, for

we have nothing which we did not receive. Associating with people of low position is a mark of humility.

Peace is not always possible in such an evil world. But we are not to produce enmity toward others. We must not avenge, for that is God's place and He does a much better job. God promises to avenge His people. He is working out His purpose in everything, so we must not personally retaliate. Some of God's power to administer justice He has delegated to civil authority (13:4). Let us treat enemies as friends, for Christ died for us when we were His enemies (Matthew 5:43-48). All of the ill will of others is made more inexcusable when we treat them well. Ancient Egyptians carried a pan of burning coals on their heads to represent the searing pain of shame, guilt, and remorse (v. 20). G. W. Carver, the great black scientist said, "I will never let another man ruin my life by making me hate him." That's what it means to overcome evil with good. It's part of the character that counts!

God and Government

The authorities that exist have been established by God.
Romans 13:1

CUBS OWNER PHIL WRIGLEY didn't do a very effective job of governing the team from 1961-65. He selected an eight-member "college of coaches" who took turns running the team. The results? The Cubs remained in or near the National League cellar during those years.

Good government is necessary in the baseball business and in nations. God has established human government to protect man from himself! He has established the good governors and the bad ones (Daniel 4; Proverbs 21:1). Jesus said that Pilate had authority from God to crucify Him (John 19:10-11). David refused to harm wicked King Saul because God had anointed him (1 Samuel 24 and 26). When Paul wrote to the Romans, the Roman Empire ruled the world with an iron fist.

Judgment from the government awaits those who rebel against it. God has given civil government the right and responsibility to exact the death penalty for certain wrong doing (Genesis 9:6). The government is an agent of God's wrath against evil. Life is precious and whoever takes someone else's life is to forfeit his own.

Governmental authority is not absolute, however. There are times to obey God and to disobey the government (Acts 4:19, 5:29). Any government that orders us to sin is not to be obeyed in that order. Such governments won't last long, for God will punish them. The function of government is to reward righteousness and to punish evil (v. 3). When any government begins to do the opposite, its days are numbered, though we may suffer until it falls — and after it falls.

Christians are to pay income taxes and import-export taxes. To refuse to pay taxes or to disrespect the government is to rebel against God (Luke 20:25). Paul wrote these words to the Romans when the government under Nero was vile, brutal, and immoral. God is serious about our respect for government, for even a bad government is better than no government! Come to think of it, we are greatly blessed to be under the American government today. It's still the best in this worl

Read Romans 13:8-14

Day Life or Night Life?

The night is nearly over; the day is almost here. So let us put aside the deeds of darkness and put on the armor of light.

Romans 13:12

WHITE SOX MANAGER JERRY MANUAL walks in the light. He is a born-again Christian who prepared for his 1997 interview with two days of fasting and prayer. At the news conference to announce his hiring, general manager Ron Schmeler recalled that "the room lit up" when Manual walked into the initial interview. Jerry believes that first impression was an answer to prayer. "When I went in there, I had a plan," he said. "God gave me a plan. It is my belief that was spiritual."

Believers in Jesus have come out of spiritual darkness into the light of God's glory. God gives us a plan for life. Once we were blind. Now, we see truth in Jesus. We are children of the day, not of the night. Light has come to dispel the darkness of this evil world system. Our lifestyle is to be pure and holy, for it is "day life" instead of "night life."

What does "day life" look like? It means we pay debts ASAP. Proverbs 22:7 says the borrower is servant to the lender. This principle would seem to prohibit profiting with someone else's money. It would seem to be a sin to remain in debt when one could get out of debt.

One debt we can never finish paying is the debt of love we owe to others. Love is a command. Loving others, believers and unbelievers, sums up several of God's commands in interpersonal relationships.

To live in "day life" we must *wake up!* It is time to be concerned for eternal things. There is a distinct line between sin and righteousness. We must stop being indifferent to sin. Jesus is coming soon. It is night time in this dark world and the days are evil (Ephesians 5:16). Man is

63

depraved and Satan dominates the world system. But Jesus' return is near! Be alert! Time is running out! Every day we are nearer our eternal home. Now is not the time to live according to this world's value system! There is only one step between us and heaven!

It is shameful to walk around in pajamas during the day. We are to "put on" the Lord Jesus Christ. We are to put aside the deeds of darkness and put on the armor of light (Ephesians 6:10-18). We all look better wearing Jesus!

Augustine was a brilliant but carnal person. When he read verse 14, God used it to convict him. His life became radically different. He has been called "Saint" Augustine since. He removed his "pajamas," put on Jesus Christ and became a child of daylight in a dark world. Have you done the same?

Conflict Unnecessary

For the kingdom of heaven is not a matter of eating and drinking, but of righteousness, peace, and joy in the Holy Spirit . . .

Romans 14:17

THE 1909 WORLD SERIES was the most violent ever played. At least a dozen players on the Tigers and Pirates were hurt. Vengeful pitches drilled 10 batters in the head and ribs. On the base paths, runners regularly slashed arms and legs of infielders. It was a Series of unnecessary conflict.

As Christians, we are to avoid unnecessary conflict, for believers in Jesus Christ are free! We are servants of the Lord Jesus Christ who has freed us from the bondage of sin and death. We are justified by faith alone, totally apart from works! Obviously, we do not desire to sin. Sin was our old master. Some things (adultery, stealing, murder) are clearly sin and to be avoided. Christians disagree about conduct not clearly spelled out in Scripture, however. Paul discusses this in Romans 14.

First, we are not to judge fellow servants on matters not covered by Scripture. Other Christians are God's servants, not ours! Each will give an account to God! The church has no authority to make rules or questions of personal liberty. Weak Christians sometimes hold on to prohibitions, superstitions, legalisms, and unbiblical taboos. Legalism is always a sign of spiritual immaturity, no matter one's age! Stronger believers who recognize we are justified by faith alone are not to dispute with weaker brothers about their unfounded scruples. In Paul's day, the issue was Jewish religious rituals that some were used to following. Whether to eat meat bought at the market (which may have been offered to an idol at a pagan temple) or whether to consider one day or every day as sacred to the Lord were debated.

Idols are nothing, but those whose conscience was bothered should not eat the meat possibly offered to them. Those who ate should not look down upon those who didn't, nor should they eat it in their presence! Weak brothers are still brothers and *weakness* is not *wickedness. Both* types of Christians are accepted by God. We don't know each other's motives. God is the one we serve and He is our judge!

Scripture is also silent about special days of the week and our activities on these days. We must respect those who worship on Saturday, Sunday and every day! Let us base our convictions upon God's Word instead of man's traditions. In matters not spelled out in Scripture, let us never violate our *convictions.* We must act in excitement, peace and joy. We must not violate our *consciences.* We must be able to look back after an activity without guilt or shame. We must not be a "stumbling block" to trip a brother (vs. 20-21) or an obstacle ("trap or snare") for a weaker brother. Sometimes we avoid an activity for the sake of others. "Mutual forbearance" is a good principle. Conflict between believers is unnecessary.

Encouragement

May the God who gives endurance and encouragement give you a spirit of unity among yourselves as you follow Christ Jesus, so that with one heart and mouth you may glorify the God and Father of our Lord Jesus Christ.

Romans 15:5-6

WHEN JOHNNY OATES managed the 1994 Baltimore Orioles, the team's owner was very critical of him. He called Johnny "a problem," "obstinate," insecure," "not a very good manager," and "not a good leader." When he was fired at the end of the season, the Texas Rangers hired him. By 1997, he was the most successful manager in Rangers' history. When that season opened, he was greeted by a huge roar of approval by 45,000 Texas fans.

"I accepted it for what it was," Oates said, — "a tribute to the team, from the ownership to the front office to the players — for what was accomplished last season. But I admit, it knocked my socks off. I don't care who you are, we all like to be appreciated."

To encourage means "to infuse with courage." God is in the business of encouragement and He desires that His followers encourage each other! How do we encourage other Christians?

First, the strong believers must bear with the overconscientious scruples of weaker believers. We must "help them bear the weight" of things they feel they must not do. Strong believers are not to please themselves by selfishly insisting on their own rights. Jesus is our example. He didn't please Himself, but He always pleased His Father. He bore the insults of others as He did so (Psalm 69:9). He even gave Himself for His enemies! He came to help others, not to help Himself (Matthew 20:28). He gave Himself for us while we were still sinners (Romans 5:8). This self-denial pleased God. Things actually go better for us and harmony is increased when we do not please ourselves first.

67

Second, we encourage others by sharing Scripture. There is no hope apart from God's Word. Vernon McGee says, "The greatest sin today is ignorance of God's Word." Both Old Testament stories and New Testament revelations teach us, produce endurance and encouragement, and result in hope during trouble and sorrow on earth. Let us labor to understand and follow the literal meaning of Scripture.

Third, we are encouraged when we understand our purpose for living: to glorify God (vs. 6, 9). When we accept others in the faith, God is glorified. Jesus accepts us and fellowships with us. He accepted Gentiles, who had been in great rebellion against God by worshipping idols of wood and stone. The unity of Jews and Gentiles under King Jesus will bring great glory to God and encouragement to us.

Encouragement (joy, peace, and hope) are all results of trusting Jesus Christ (v. 13). Why do so many folks have no encouragement today? They refuse to trust Jesus. He is the author and object of encouragement! When we spread Jesus and His Word we spread encouragement!

Paul's Plans

It has always been my ambition to preach the gospel where Christ was not known, so that I would not be building on someone else's foundation.

Romans 15:20

BO JACKSON had a plan on July 7, 1987. As an outfielder for the Royals, Bo decided to play pro football as a "hobby." A former Heisman Trophy winner, he signed a five-year, $7.4 million contract with the L. A. Raiders, becoming the highest paid non-quarterback at that time.

Like Bo Jackson, Paul had a plan and he was very straight forward in writing to the Roman believers. At the same time, he had a deep respect for their spiritual maturity (v. 14). He didn't boast of his own achievements or miracles performed, but only of what Christ had accomplished through him. He had won many to Christ who had moved to Rome, so in one sense, he had founded the Roman church.

Paul always desired to preach Christ where no one else had done it, where witchcraft and idolatry had reigned for ages. He was an "ice-breaker" for Christ. Now, Paul has another plan. He was taking a financial gift from Gentile Christians in Greece to poor Jewish Christians in Jerusalem. There was famine in Judea and persecution of Christians, too. He wanted prayers for safety because Jewish religious zealots (like Paul used to be!) were a real danger. They hated Christians, especially Jewish Christians!

After going to Jerusalem, Paul planned to go to Spain via Rome and visit the Romans to whom he was writing.

What happened? Were Paul's plans fulfilled? Yes and no! Paul was arrested in Jerusalem and appealed to the Caesar. He spent two years in jail in Caesarea, along the Mediterranean coast. His ship was wrecked in a storm and he arrived to Rome in chains. He got to Rome, but not as he planned. We don't know if he went on to Spain, but if so he was rearrested before being beheaded in a Roman prison.

It is wise to plan and plan we must. But things don't always happen according to our plans. Man proposes but God disposes! Our lives rest in the sovereign will and purpose of our Creator!

Paul — A "People Person"

Everyone has heard of your obedience, so I am full of joy over you; but I want you to be wise about what is good, and innocent about what is evil.

Romans 16:19

RELIEF PITCHER JERRY DIPOTO echoed the feelings of many players when he announced his retirement in March, 2001. "The hardest part for me was the understanding that I wouldn't be in the clubhouse and I wouldn't be on the field any more," he said. Clearly, most players enjoy the camaraderie and closeness of people on teams as much as they thrive on competition.

Paul was also a "people person." He was personable and personal. As he concluded his longest and most complete letter, he personally greeted 27 people in Rome. Though he had never been to the city, he knew these people from contacts in other areas of the world. He remembered names and faces! He also sent greetings from eight others with whom he had recent contact. Some of Paul's friends were prominent, some public officials, and some related to him. Phoebe, whose name means "radiant," was a prominent Christian businesswoman who carried Paul's letter to Rome on a business trip.

Because people mattered, Paul warned the Roman Christians about false teachers who would try to divide them. Anyone who teaches contrary to Scripture is a false teacher and is to be shunned (v. 17). Believers in Jesus are to be wise as serpents and harmless as doves as they examine what is taught. False teachers serve themselves. They use smooth talk and flattery to deceive naïve people (v. 18). It is false teachers, not those who leave churches to avoid them, that are guilty of causing division. Knowledge of Scripture is a safeguard against them.

Inning #9

The Winning Run

PERHAPS YOU HAVE READ this book but never personally trusted the Savior with your earthly life and your
eternal destiny. The following baseball illustration explains
how you can come to know the Lord Jesus Christ:

In baseball, a runner must touch all four bases to
score a run for his team. The path to abundant and eternal life is very similar to the base paths on a ball diamond.

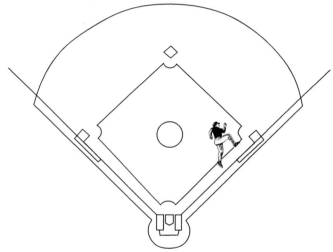

Step 1 (FIRST BASE) along that path is realizing that God
cares about you. He not only created you, but He also
loves you very deeply. He is seeking to give you an abundant life now and for eternity.

*For God so loved the world that He gave His one and only
Son, that whoever believes in Him shall not perish but
have eternal life.*

John 3:16

*I have come that they may have life, and have it to the
full.*

John 10:10

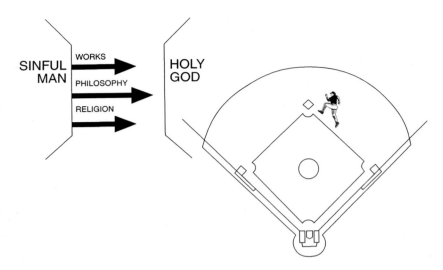

At SECOND BASE (step 2), we admit that we are sinners and separated from God. He is perfect, pure, and good; we are not. Because by nature we disobey Him and resist Him, He cannot have fellowship with us without denying His goodness and holiness. Instead, He must judge us.

Whoever believes in Him is not condemned; but whoever does not believe stands condemned already, because he has not believed in the name of God's one and only Son.
John 3:18

We realize we can never reach God through our own efforts. They do not solve the problem of our sin.

For all have sinned and come short of the glory of God.
Romans 3:23

But your iniquities have separated you from your God; your sins have hidden His face from you, so that He will not hear.
Isaiah 59:2

For the wages of sin is death, but the gift of God is eternal life in Christ Jesus our Lord.
Romans 6:23

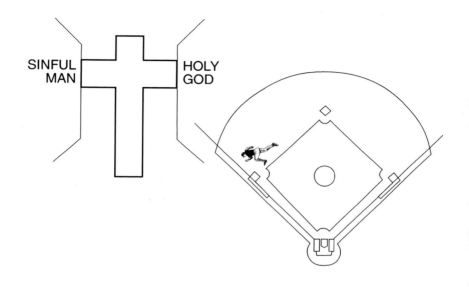

THIRD BASE is so close to scoring. Here (step 3) we under-stand that God has sent His Son, Jesus Christ, to die on the cross in payment for our sins. By His sacrifice, we may advance Home.

But God demonstrates His own love for us in this: While we were still sinners, Christ died for us.

Romans 5:8

For Christ died for sins once for all, the righteous for the unrighteous, to bring you to God.

I Peter 3:18

Jesus answered, "I am the way and the truth and the life. No one comes to the Father except through Me."

John 14:6

However, being CLOSE to Home does NOT count!

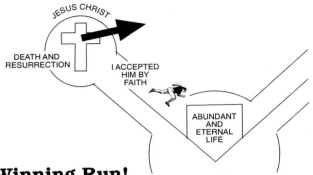

The Winning Run!

To score (step 4), we must personally receive Jesus
Christ as Savior and Lord of our lives. We must not only
realize that He died to rescue people from their sin but
we must also trust Him to rescue us from our own sin.
We cannot "squeeze" ourselves home any other way, and
He will not force Himself upon us.

*Yet to all who received Him, to those who believed in His
name, He gave the right to become children of God.*
John 1:12

*For it is by grace you have been saved, through faith —
and this is not from yourselves, it is the gift of God — not
by works, so that no one can boast.*
Ephesians 2:8-9

Why not receive Jesus Christ as your Savior and Lord
right now? Simply say: "Yes, Lord," to His offer to forgive
you for your sins and to change you.

_____

(signed)

_____

(date)

Tell someone of your decision and keep studying God's
Word. These things greatly strengthen you (Romans
10:9-10). You may write CROSS TRAINING PUBLISHING for
further encouragement. We would be thrilled to hear of
your commitment! Welcome to eternal life!

CROSS TRAINING PUBLISHING

P.O. Box 1541

Grand Island, NE 68802

An Extra Inning

The Perfect Reliever

THE FOLLOWING BASEBALL illustration explains how to walk consistently in the power of the Holy Spirit, our only hope for victory in spiritual warfare.

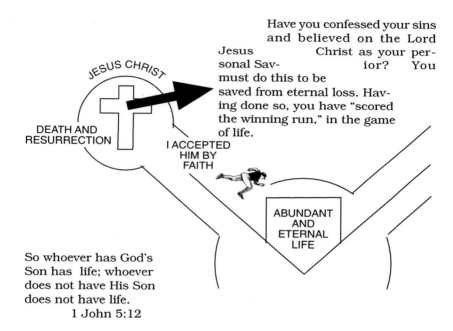

Have you confessed your sins and believed on the Lord Jesus Christ as your personal Savior? You must do this to be saved from eternal loss. Having done so, you have "scored the winning run," in the game of life.

JESUS CHRIST

DEATH AND RESURRECTION

I ACCEPTED HIM BY FAITH

ABUNDANT AND ETERNAL LIFE

So whoever has God's Son has life; whoever does not have His Son does not have life.
1 John 5:12

YOU SIGNED WITH THE WINNING TEAM WHEN YOU RECEIVED CHRIST!

1. Your sins were forgiven (Colossians 1:14).
2. You became a child of God (John 1:12).
3. God indwelt you with His Spirit so you may live victoriously over the world (John 15:18-19), the flesh (Romans 7:15-18), and the devil (1 Peter 5:8).
4. You began the process of discovering God's purpose for your life (Romans 8:29).

BUT. . . .WHAT'S HAPPENING NOW?

Though our Lord has assured all His children of eternal life (John 10:28) and our position in Christ never changes, our practice may sometimes bring dishonor to God. The enemy rally makes life miserable.

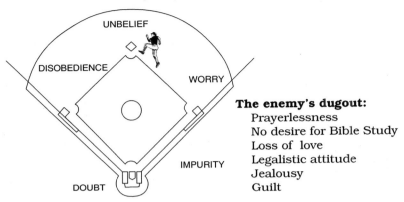

The enemy's dugout:
Prayerlessness
No desire for Bible Study
Loss of love
Legalistic attitude
Jealousy
Guilt

This rally must be stopped, for the Bible makes it clear that no one who belongs to God can continually practice sin (I John 2:3; 3:6-10).

These two pitchers' mounds represent the two lifestyles from which a Christian must choose:

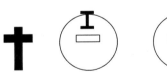

Self in control of the game and Christ's Resurrection power waiting in the bullpen — enemy rally produces discord.

For we naturally love to do evil things that are just the opposite from the things that the Holy Spirit tells us to do;

Power of Christ replaces self on the mound — rally is stopped and peace is restored.

. . . and the good things we want to do when the Spirit has His way with us are just the opposite of our natural desires.
Galatians 5:17a

SO, WHAT'S THE SOLUTION?

76

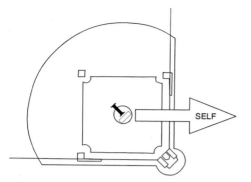

BRING IN THE PERFECT RELIEVER!

We must step off the mound and allow God to have complete authority by giving control of the game to the Holy Spirit.

Only by giving the Holy Spirit of God His rightful place of authority over our every thought, word and deed, can we consistently overcome defeat and despair.

If we are living now by the Holy Spirit's power, let us follow the Holy Spirit's leading in every part of our lives (Galatians 5:25).

WHAT DOES THE HOLY SPIRIT DO?

When you received Jesus Christ as Savior, the Holy Spirit *indwelt* you (Romans 8:9). Though all who have received Christ are indwelt by the Spirit, not all are *filled* (empowered, motivated) by the Spirit.

The Holy Spirit:
a. Instructs us in all things (John 14:25-27).
b. Always glorifies Jesus Christ (John 15:26; 16:13-15).
c. Convicts us when things are wrong in our lives. (John 16:7-8).
d. Helps us to share Christ with others (Acts 1:8).
e. Assures us we belong to Christ (Romans 8:26).
f. Enables us to live above circumstances through prayer (Romans 8:26).
g. Flows from us as the source of an abundant and victorious life. (John 7:37-39).

HOW CAN YOU BE FILLED?

You can be filled (motivated) by the Holy Spirit right now IF YOU ARE WILLING to step off the mound of your life and give the ball to the Master Coach.

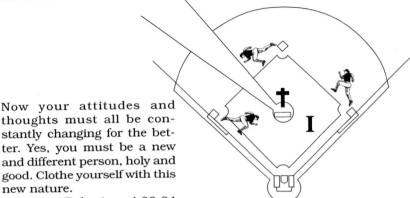

Now your attitudes and thoughts must all be constantly changing for the better. Yes, you must be a new and different person, holy and good. Clothe yourself with this new nature.
Ephesians 4:23-24

The Master Coach will not replace you on the mound against your heart's desire. Just as in receiving Christ, living consistently in His power is a matter of your will.

The Keys to Victory: Romans 6 (NAS)

A. KNOWING THIS, that our old self was crucified with Him that our body of sin might be done away with, that we should no longer be slaves to sin; for he who has died is freed from sin! (vs. 6-7)

B. Even so, CONSIDER YOURSELVES TO BE DEAD to sin, but alive to God in Christ Jesus. (v. 11)

C. But PRESENT YOURSELVES TO GOD as those alive from the dead, and your members as instruments of righteousness to God. (v. 13b)

PRESENT YOURSELF TO GOD
THROUGH PRAYER

HERE IS A SUGGESTED PRAYER:

Dear Father,
I confess that I have taken control of my life and therefore have sinned against You. Thank You for forgiving me. I now CONSIDER myself dead to sin and PRESENT this body to You as a living sacrifice. I desire to be filled with Your Spirit as I live in obedience to Your WORD. Thank You for taking control of my life by the power of Your Spirit.

Amen.

HOW DO YOU KNOW YOU ARE FILLED BY THE HOLY SPIRIT?

 And we are sure of this, that He WILL listen to us whenever we ask Him for ANYTHING IN LINE WITH HIS WILL. And if we really KNOW He is listening when we talk to Him and make our requests, then we CAN BE SURE that He will answer us.   1 John 5:14-15

Is it God's will that you be filled (motivated) by His Spirit? He has said so (Ephesians 5:18). Therefore, based upon the authority of God's Word and His trustworthiness, you can KNOW you are filled with His Spirit regardless of your emotions.

WHAT WILL GOD'S PERFECT RELIEVER ACCOMPLISH IN YOUR LIFE?

He will retire all doubt, fear, worry and other sins that run the bases of your life. He will substitute love, joy, peace and other fruits (Galatians 5:22-23). His assortment of pitches includes truth, faith, righteousness and other weapons through which daily victory is assured (Ephesians 6:10-18). He will turn your eyes to the Master Coach, Jesus Christ, and conform you to His likeness (II Corinthians 3:18). You can praise and thank God through trials and suffering in the game of life, knowing He has a plan for you (James 1:2-4). The final score will bring much glory to God!

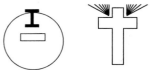

WHAT IF SELF TRIES TO GET BACK INTO THE GAME?

The self life is a deadly enemy of the control of the Holy Spirit. Often self will try to return to the game, and when that happens, Satan quickly reloads the bases. If you sense this happening, take these steps:

1) Confess all known sin to God and thank Him. He has forgiven you (1 John 1:9).

2) Trust Christ to again fill you with the Holy Spirit, Who will once more take control (Ephesians 5:18).

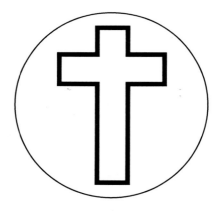

PLAYING THE GAME OF LIFE under His control will become a way of life, and you will experience constant victory! If "The Perfect Reliever" has been of help to you, please share it with a friend who also knows Jesus Christ as his personal Savior. He, too, can enjoy walking daily in the power of the Holy Spirit. May God bless you.

Elliot Johnson

For further information, please write:

Cross Training Publishing
P.O. Box 1541
Grand Island, NE 68802